9/02

IN AMERICAN HISTORY

THE PONY EXPRESS IN AMERICAN HISTORY

Anita Louise McCormick

Enslow Publishers, Inc.

40 Industrial Road   PO Box 38
Box 398   Aldershot
Berkeley Heights, NJ 07922   Hants GU12 6BP
USA   UK

http://www.enslow.com

Library of Congress Cataloging-in-Publication Data

McCormick, Anita Louise.
   The Pony express in American history / Anita Louise McCormick.
      p. cm. — (In American history)
   Includes bibliographical references (p.) and index.
   ISBN 0-7660-1296-4
   1. Pony express—History—Juvenile literature. 2. Postal service—United
States—History—Juvenile literature. 3. West (U.S.)—History—
1860–1890—Juvenile literature. [1. Pony express. 2. West (U.S.)—
History.] I. Title. II. Series.

HE6375.P65 M234   2001
383'.143'0973—dc21
                                                00-010156

Printed in the United States of America

10 9 8 7 6 5 4 3 2 1

To Our Readers: All Internet Addresses in this book were active and appropriate
at the time we went to press. Any comments or suggestions can be sent by e-mail
to Comments@enslow.com or to the address on the back cover.

Illustration Credits: Enslow Publishers, Inc., pp. 12, 42; Henry T.
Williams, *The Pacific Tourist*, 1876, pp. 6, 44, 70, 86; John Grafton, *The
American West in the Nineteenth Century* (New York: Dover Publications,
Inc., 1992), pp. 21, 90; National Archives, pp. 19, 26, 64, 77, 84, 87;
National Park Service, p. 55; Reproduced from the *Dictionary of
American Portraits*, Published by Dover Publications, Inc., in 1967, pp.
9, 39.

Cover Illustrations: Henry T. Williams, *The Pacific Tourist*, 1876;
Reproduced from the *Dictionary of American Portraits*, Published by
Dover Publications, Inc., in 1967.

★ CONTENTS ★

1 Here Comes the
Pony Express! 5

2 The Nation Expands
to the West 8

3 Mail Contracts to the West 24

4 The Pony Express
Is Established 35

5 The First Ride of
the Pony Express 51

6 The Lives of Pony
Express Riders 60

7 The Final Months of
the Pony Express 74

8 Legacy of the Pony Express 89

Timeline 93

Chapter Notes 95

Further Reading 100

Internet Addresses 101

Index 103

HERE COMES THE PONY EXPRESS!

In 1861, writer Mark Twain decided to take a trip across the American West by horse-drawn coach. Twain, like many other western travelers of the time, hoped he would have the opportunity to see a rider for the Pony Express streak across the plains. If travelers were so fortunate, they knew that they would have an intriguing story to tell all their family and friends when they returned from their western trip—a story that would keep everyone glued to their chairs.

When the coach driver exclaimed, "Here he comes!" Twain and his fellow passengers knew they were about to witness one of the most exciting events of the mid-nineteenth century—the legendary run of the Pony Express.

Even those passengers who had been sleeping jumped to attention. They immediately started to scan the horizon, looking for the Pony Express mail rider who was coming rapidly in their direction. Twain described what happened next:

A Pony Express rider is seen here, hurrying along his route.

Every neck stretched further, and every eye strained wider. Away across the endless dead level of the prairie a black spot appears against the sky, and it is plain that it moves. . . . In a second or two it becomes a horse and a rider, rising and falling . . . growing more and more distinct, more and more sharply defined—nearer and still nearer, and the flutter of the hoofs comes faintly to the ear—another instant a whoop and a hurrah . . . and man and horse burst past our excited faces, and go winging away like a belated fragment of a storm![1]

Mark Twain was not alone in his admiration of the brave young riders who raced across the West. At the time of Twain's trip, the entire nation was abuzz with excitement over a new mail-delivery service called the Pony Express.

In the years before telegraph lines or train tracks connected California, Utah, and other western territories to the East, the Pony Express was a daring venture. It provided fast, dependable mail service to America's developing West. Its route stretched approximately 1,966 miles through the center of the nation, between St. Joseph, Missouri, and Sacramento, California.

Before the Pony Express, letters from the East often took a month or more to reach California. The majority of letters to the West were transported by steamship, private delivery services, or by stagecoach on John Butterfield's "Ox Bow Route," which dipped far into the Southern part of the nation. But once Pony Express service began in April 1860, letters could be transported from St. Joseph, Missouri, to Sacramento, California, in a little over a week. By today's standards, this might sound slow. But in the early 1860s, it seemed miraculous.

Pony Express riders bravely faced danger on every mail run. With each load of mail they carried across the deserts, mountains, and plains of the West, they performed a service that was vital to the nation. They helped keep distant family members connected, and they brought America's West into contact with the rest of the nation at a time when the country was about to be torn apart by the Civil War. No matter what dangers Pony Express riders might have to face, they always remembered their motto: "The mail must go through."[2]

2

THE NATION EXPANDS TO THE WEST

When the American government bought new lands to the west of the Mississippi River in the early 1800s and opened them for settlement, many people decided to seek their fortunes in the West. Land was much less expensive there than it was in the East. In some areas, land was free to anyone who was willing to go and claim it.

Up to that time, most new settlements were built near existing communities. So it was not a problem to obtain food and other supplies. However, settlers who chose to move west were faced with problems that few Americans had experienced recently. People were settling in isolated communities, cut off from the rest of the nation. If food and other supplies could not be produced locally, they had to be transported from communities hundreds, if not thousands, of miles away. This was often expensive and impractical.

Settlers who had moved west in the early to mid-1800s were frustrated with the lack of communication with the East. Businessmen in the West could not obtain information on prices of goods or product-and-supply shipments until it was a month or more out of date. Ordinary citizens were affected as well. Farmers, miners, and other settlers were frustrated by having to wait for months to hear from loved ones back east. Thousands who went west by wagon train had no way to get word back to their families.

Historian Alvin F. Harlow wrote, "From 1800 to the present time the cry in America has been, 'Faster! Faster!'"[1] But for many years, no one was able to find a way to deliver mail to the West in a way that was both economical and efficient.

Calhoun Pushes for Better Mail Service

John Calhoun, a congressman from South Carolina, recognized how important it was to maintain rapid and dependable communications across the country. While this was true of the entire nation, it was especially important to the development of the West. A better system of roads would speed the delivery

Southern Congressman John C. Calhoun was one of the first to push for faster mail service to the West.

of mail. It would also lower prices for transporting food and other products.

In 1817, Calhoun pushed for a bill that would use money from the United States Treasury to build a system of roads and canals across the nation. This, Calhoun felt, was the best way to bridge the gap between the West and the rest of the nation. In a speech that year, Calhoun said,

> Whatever . . . impedes the intercourse [communication] of the extremes with this, the centre of the Republic [Washington, D.C.] weakens the Union. Let us then . . . bind the Republic together with a perfect system of roads and canals. Let us conquer space. It is thus the most distant parts of the Republic will be brought within a few days travel of the centre; it is thus that a citizen of the West will read the news of Boston still moist from the press. The mail and the press . . . are the nerves of the body politic. By them the slightest impression made on the most remote parts is communicated to the whole system.[2]

Calhoun's bill passed through Congress. But President James Madison vetoed it. He did not believe that the United States Constitution allowed federal money to be spent for such projects.

During the 1830s and 1840s, the United States acquired even more land from American Indian tribes. They also won California and other western territories in a war with Mexico. With all this new land available, huge numbers of Americans decided to pack their belongings and move west.

SOURCE DOCUMENT

I AM NOT UNAWARE OF THE GREAT IMPORTANCE OF ROADS AND CANALS AND THE IMPROVED NAVIGATION OF WATER COURSES, AND THAT A POWER IN THE NATIONAL LEGISLATURE TO PROVIDE FOR THEM MIGHT BE EXERCISED WITH SIGNAL ADVANTAGE TO THE GENERAL PROSPERITY. BUT SEEING THAT SUCH A POWER IS NOT EXPRESSLY GIVEN BY THE CONSTITUTION . . . I HAVE NO OPTION BUT TO WITHHOLD MY SIGNATURE FROM IT. . . .[3]

President James Madison vetoed Calhoun's bill to improve transportation and communication to the West because he believed Congress lacked the power under the Constitution to handle such internal improvements.

But while people were moving to the Far West, the lands between Missouri and the Far West were mostly unoccupied by white settlers. On some maps, this region was labeled "The Great American Desert." This vast expanse included plains, deserts, and rugged mountain ranges. Travelers going west had to be constantly on guard for bandits and hostile American Indians who did not want white people to pass uninvited through their territory. All these factors made transportation and communication with the West difficult.

In 1845, President James K. Polk discovered that it took six months to get an important message to the California Territory. By then, it was becoming obvious to many government officials that a faster means of

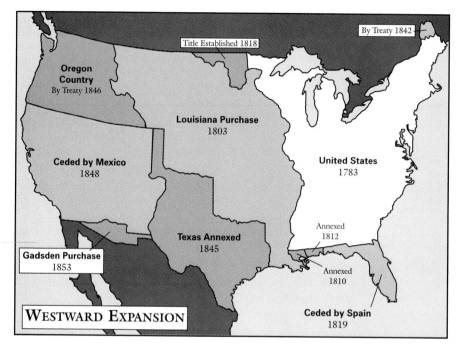

Title Established 1818

By Treaty 1842

Oregon
Country
By Treaty 1846

Louisiana Purchase
1803

Ceded by Mexico
1848

United States
1783

Annexed
1812

Texas Annexed
1845

Gadsden Purchase
1853

Annexed
1810

WESTWARD EXPANSION

Ceded by Spain
1819

Through the first half of the nineteenth century, the United States expanded as it acquired new lands in the West.

communicating with the West was needed. Congress tried to find an economical way to provide reliable mail service to military officials, government leaders, businessmen, miners, farmers, and others who lived thousands of miles from the major population centers of the East.

Steamships Carry Mail to the West

In March 1847, Congress passed a bill that called for five steamships to be built to carry mail to California and the West. Mail would be carried by ship from the northeast to New Orleans, Louisiana, then down to the Isthmus of Panama. From there, it would be transported across thirty miles of land. From the western coast of Panama, the mail would be loaded onto another steamship and taken to Oregon, where it would be distributed to settlers in the western territories. Once a month, the mail was to be transported over this route by private contractors. The plan would cost the United States government $199,000 per year.

Almost from the beginning, the steamship service ran into problems. Travel through Panama was difficult. Much of the land was covered with dense jungle. On the first steamship mail delivery to the West, in 1849, the crew abandoned ship in San Francisco to join miners looking for gold. The ship could not return to Panama until a new crew could be found. This delayed the return trip for several weeks.

To people living in the port cities of California, Steamer Day—the day the steamship arrived with mail from the East—was one of the most important holidays of the year. Often, people would line up outside of the post office hours before the ship that carried mail was due to arrive. Many times, the men who carried sacks of mail from the ship had to force their way through crowds of people who could hardly wait to find out if there were any news from home.

But while this system offered some improvement, it was still very slow. It took at least twenty-five days for the mail to go from the east coast to the west coast.

The Gold Rush Brings Thousands to California

When the United States acquired California in a treaty with Mexico in 1848, only about fourteen thousand American settlers lived there. Many farmed or ran small businesses that served the local population.

On January 24, 1848, gold was discovered at Sutter's Mill in northern California. John Sutter wanted to keep the discovery a secret, but word of the find began to spread across the country. Many people who lived in California caught "gold fever." People from all walks of life left farms and businesses with hopes of finding

SOURCE DOCUMENT

... I WENT DOWN AS USUAL, AND AFTER SHUTTING OFF THE WATER . . . , I STEPPED INTO IT, NEAR THE LOWER END, AND THERE, UPON THE ROCK, ABOUT SIX INCHES BENEATH THE SURFACE OF THE WATER, I DISCOVERED THE GOLD. I WAS ENTIRELY ALONE AT THE TIME. I PICKED UP ONE OR TWO PIECES AND EXAMINED THEM ATTENTIVELY; AND HAVING SOME GENERAL KNOWLEDGE OF MINERALS, I COULD NOT CALL TO MIND MORE THAN TWO WHICH ANY WAY RESEMBLED THIS—SULPHURET OF IRON, VERY BRIGHT AND BRITTLE; AND GOLD, BRIGHT YET MALLEABLE; I THEN TRIED IT BETWEEN TWO ROCKS, AND FOUND THAT IT COULD BE BEATEN INTO A DIFFERENT SHAPE, BUT NOT BROKEN. I THEN COLLECTED FOUR OR FIVE PIECES AND WENT UP TO MR. SCOTT . . . AND SAID, "I HAVE FOUND IT."[4]

James Marshall gave this account of discovering gold at Sutter's Mill.

enough gold to make them wealthy. They headed for any stream or piece of land that held the promise of riches. On May 29, 1849, the San Francisco *Californian* newspaper announced that it was suspending publication because there were not enough employees to run it. Even the printer had left town in search of gold. An article in the *Californian*'s final issue said,

> The whole country, from San Francisco to Los Angeles, and from the sea shore to the base of the Sierra Nevada, resounds with the . . . cry of gold, gold, gold,—while the field is left half planted, the house half built, and everything neglected but the manufacture of shovels and picks, and the means of transportation to the spot where one man obtained $128 [this was over a month's pay at the time] of the real stuff in one day's washing. . . .[5]

In December 1848, President Polk mentioned the discovery of gold at Sutter's Mill in a message to Congress. Within a year of the discovery, more than one hundred thousand people from the East went to California in search of gold. But not everyone went to look for gold. Many people went to California to run businesses, ranches, and farms. When a census was taken a little over ten years later, the population of the California Territory had risen to three hundred eighty thousand. By 1860, California's population had risen to nearly half a million and the territory had become a state.

California was isolated from the populated eastern half of the nation. It was expensive and time-consuming to ship products more than two thousand miles across the plains and mountains of the West. Much of the food, as well as many products and services that Californians needed, had to be supplied locally. As the western population increased and the number of businesses and farms in the region grew, they were able to supply most of the western population's needs.

However, people living in California and other western territories such as Utah, Nevada, and Oregon still had one serious problem. They did not have dependable communication. In the mid-1800s, mail service in the East was usually fast and dependable. But letters that had to be transported between California, Oregon, or other western regions and the East could take weeks, if not months, to arrive.

The number of post offices in the United States nearly doubled between 1845 and 1860. And nearly one hundred thousand miles of new postal roads were built between 1845 and 1869. However, the majority of improvements in postal service that were made during the 1840s and 1850s only benefited people living in the eastern and central sections of the country. Americans who had settled in the West were still forced to deal with slow and unreliable mail service.

The Need for Better Communication

Pennsylvania Senator Richard Brodhead understood how serious the problem was. He said, "Historians have informed us that mountains make enemies of people who would otherwise be friends. We have a vast range of mountains and a great desert between our Pacific possessions and the Atlantic States. . . . if we are to live in peace together, we must have rapid communication."[6]

Businessmen, ordinary citizens, and government and military officials in the West were troubled by this problem. In the years before the Internet, telephones, telegraph, and other electronic forms of communication, letters were the only way people could communicate over great distances. For people living in the West, receiving a letter from home was the only way of keeping in touch.

In 1849, Reverend William Taylor explained the important role mail delivery played in the lives of western settlers. He said,

> The greatest local attraction [in San Francisco] . . . is the post office. Thousands of men here . . . never were absent from their wives and children a week at any one time, till they started for California. . . . How desolate [empty] the hearts of these different classes of men. . . . The only substitutes [for loved ones] for them were the little drops and glimpses of social life and light obtained through the post office.[7]

At that time, nearly everyone agreed that the United States government would have to provide the funding necessary before mail service to the Far West could be improved.[8] The project was too expensive and risky to interest private investors. So western businessmen and government officials pressured Congress to offer payments to companies that were willing to make these improvements.

One possible solution was to build a transcontinental railroad. In 1853 and 1854, the United States government studied five routes to determine "the most practicable and economical route for a Railroad from the Mississippi River to the Pacific."[9] Each study team reported that the line it had surveyed was the best. Jefferson Davis was the secretary of war at the time. A Southerner, Davis supported the southernmost route. But rivalry between the North and the South resulting from disagreement over slavery and states' rights was already building. This made it difficult for Congress to agree on which route to use. As a result, action on the project was delayed for nearly a decade.[10]

Private Express Companies

The United States Postal Service only carried mail to a limited number of locations in the West. San Diego, San Francisco, and Monterey were the primary mail centers in California. But many people lived in mining camps hundreds of miles away from these coastal mail centers. By the time a miner received a letter from home, it was often three to four months old.

From the mid-1800s, privately owned express companies played an important role in distributing the mail. If not for riders from private express companies delivering mail to small towns and mining camps, many settlers would have had no mail service at all.

Most early express companies were small operations. Alexander H. Todd, for example, started a one-man express service in 1849. Todd had come to

Jefferson Davis, as secretary of war, pushed for the southernmost railroad route. A devoted Southerner, Davis would later become the president of the Confederacy during the Civil War.

California in search of gold, but he soon realized that he could make more money delivering mail. Todd charged men who worked in western mines one dollar to register for his delivery service. His fee for delivering each letter on horseback was one ounce of gold dust. For delivery of a newspaper, the cost was two ounces of gold dust. Once they were on Todd's list, miners were able to receive any mail that arrived in their name at the San Francisco, Sacramento, or Stockton post offices.[11]

Alonzo Delano, the owner of a private express company in the mid-1800s, described what happened in the California mining camps when mail arrived: "The Express has arrived! Every pick and shovel is dropped, every pan is laid aside, every rocker is stopped with its half-washed dirt, every claim is deserted, and they crowd around with eager inquiries, 'Have you got a letter for me?'"[12]

Within a few years, a network of privately owned express lines stretched from Mexico to Canada. Companies such as Yankee Jim's Express, Loon Creek Express, Blackfoot Express, and Salmon River and Nez Perces Express provided mail service between every major town and mining camp in the West.

There was such a large market for mail delivery in the West that several wealthy businessmen became interested in financing express mail ventures. Weld & Company was organized in 1849. Adams and Company started business in 1850. And Wells, Fargo & Company, which already ran an express service in the

Gold mining could be a dangerous business. Miners had to face not only the loneliness of isolation and the hardships of frontier conditions, but also the possibility of encountering hostile creatures, such as bears.

East, expanded its service into California in 1852.[13] These larger express mail companies were able to cover more territory and carry larger amounts of mail than much of their competition. But even with these improvements, many areas of the West lacked fast, dependable mail service.

The Government Forces Express Companies to Charge Postage

Even though the United States government was unwilling to spend the money necessary to build more post offices in California, it wanted income from all the mail that was delivered in the area. Even express riders who did not use the service of the United States post office were required to charge customers not only their own fees, but also the amount of postage required by the United States government.

Having to pay double postage for letters sent through private express companies angered many Californians, who were already disgusted with the poor mail service the government provided. A California newspaper in July 1855 said,

> . . . The Post Office system, as far as California is concerned, is a humbug of a nuisance. It does not facilitate intercourse between different parts of the state, but impedes it. It subjects correspondents to an onerous tax, if they select a more speedy and sure conveyance for their letters than the [government-run] mail. . . . The Express willingly carry letters for a bit each, to the Atlantic States, and we believe they would for less if they could have the entire business. . . .[14]

Most western settlers had spent at least part of their lives in the eastern states, where mail delivery was much faster and more dependable. Many hoped that railroads would soon be built to bring mail and passengers to their region. But until that was possible, they felt it was the United States government's responsibility to fund a regularly scheduled mail coach service to keep them in contact with friends, family, and business partners in the East.

3

MAIL CONTRACTS TO THE WEST

Just three years after gold was discovered, California had a population of more than three hundred thousand. In 1850, it had become a state. Still, the United States government had built only sixty post offices in California. This was not nearly enough to serve the hundreds of towns and mining camps throughout California and other parts of the West. Although private express companies also helped distribute mail to small towns and mining camps, the system was far from perfect. Many areas still had no dependable mail service.

Overland Mail Delivery

The United States government first experimented with delivery of overland mail west of the Missouri River when it awarded a contract to Samuel Woodson in 1850. The contract called for the mail to be carried once a month by horse-drawn carriage from Missouri to Salt Lake City, Utah. But Woodson ran into many difficulties. Because of bad weather, conflicts with American Indian tribes, and other unexpected problems, it was impossible for Woodson to maintain a regular schedule.

The government struggled to provide effective mail service to the West. But it was difficult to come up with a workable plan. In 1855, Congress spent $30,000 to investigate the idea of using camels to carry mail from Texas to California. Because much of the Southwest is desert, they thought camels—desert animals—might be better able to travel in the West than horses. However, mail delivery by camels proved to be impractical, and the idea was soon abandoned.

Many western settlers had traveled to California and Oregon in covered wagons. Even though the wagon trains that passed overland to the West had to deal with severe weather and Indian attacks, the overland route was shorter than any other—such as the steamship route through Panama—currently in use. It seemed to make sense for mail to be transported on the overland trail as well.[1]

In 1858, the government awarded a $190,000-a-year contract for the mail route that ran from Missouri to Salt Lake City to the firm of Hockaday and Liggett. The firm was to carry the mail over this route once a week. But it ran into the same problems that Woodson had encountered eight years earlier.

A year later, Hockaday and Liggett decided to sell its contract to deliver mail in the West. The contract was purchased by the freight and transportation firm

Most early settlers to the West moved by wagon train in large groups, although the wagons could easily be lost or destroyed along the difficult trails west.

of Russell, Majors & Waddell. At this time, Russell, Majors & Waddell was already well-known throughout the nation as a dependable firm. Because of its reputation, the firm had already been awarded government contracts for transporting 16 million pounds of supplies to military posts throughout the West.

To carry out this contract, Russell, Majors & Waddell put to work forty thousand oxen, one thousand mules, thirty-five hundred to four thousand wagons, and more than four thousand men. This, in addition to its private freight service business, required the firm to have approximately seventy-five thousand oxen available for use.[2]

SOURCE DOCUMENT

[T]HE GREAT DIFFICULTY IS TO GET THERE, FOR THE ROAD IS LONG AND DANGEROUS. . . . THE SCENE WE WITNESSED ON THE ROAD PRESENTED INDEED A MELANCHOLY PROOF OF THE UNCERTAINTY WHICH ATTENDS OUR HIGHEST PROSPECTS IN LIFE. THE BLEACHED BONES OF ANIMALS EVERYWHERE STREWED ALONG THE TRACK, THE HASTILY ERECTED MOUND, BENEATH WHICH LIE THE REMAINS OF SOME DEPARTED FRIEND OR RELATIVE . . . [T]HE NUMEROUS SHATTERED FRAGMENTS OF THE VEHICLES, PROVISION, TOOLS, ETC., INTENDED TO BE TAKEN ACROSS THESE WILD PLAINS, TELL US ANOTHER TALE OF RECKLESS BOLDNESS WITH WHICH MANY ENTERED UPON THIS HAPHAZARD ENTERPRISE.[3]

Father Pierre-Jean de Smet wrote this letter describing the hardships of traveling to settle in the West in 1852.

The Post Office Appropriations Bill

Until the late 1850s, people who lived west of Salt Lake City, Utah, had no dependable way of exchanging letters with their friends, family, and business connections in the East. Fear of attacks by American Indians, extreme weather conditions in the deserts and mountains, and the high cost of dealing with these problems kept most private businesses from attempting to start such a service. Some lawmakers, including Senator William Gwin of California, pushed for the government to build roads to the West. Such roads, he argued, would not only improve mail service, but they would also benefit the military in transporting men, guns, and other supplies to the West in the event of war. But legislators did not want to spend the money, and the plan was rejected.

But as the population of the West increased, the government was finally pressured to take action. In 1856, approximately seventy-five thousand Californians signed a petition to Congress demanding better mail service. That year, a Post Office Appropriations Bill passed through Congress. The bill included an amendment that provided for overland mail delivery to the West. The mail was to be taken west in four-horse coaches that had room for six passengers, along with three bags of letters and one bag of newspapers. However, the amendment did not specify which route the contractor would take.[4]

Russell, Majors, Waddell, and several other businessmen who had experience in the transportation field entered bids to transport mail via the Central Overland Route—a route that cut across the center of the nation. John Butterfield, however, entered a bid to carry the mail on a route that went deep into the Southern part of the nation.

At that time, Southern politicians had enough influence in Washington, D.C., to insist that most government mail contracts be given to companies that used southwestern trails. Because of this, all bids to carry mail on the central route were discarded. John Butterfield and his Overland Mail Company won the government contract.

The Butterfield Route

The route Butterfield proposed was approximately twenty-eight hundred miles long. This route, known as the Ox Bow Route because it was shaped like a yoke used for oxen, ran from St. Louis, Missouri, and Fort Smith, Arkansas, to San Francisco, California. It reached its destination via El Paso, Texas. Using this route, it took three to four weeks to get mail from the Missouri River to California by stagecoach.

When Northerners discovered that the new mail route ran through the Southern part of the nation, they demanded that Congress set up an alternate route that ran through the central part of the country. This was an important issue. Many people believed that the route used to deliver mail by stagecoach would be the same route that would eventually be used by the transcontinental railroad.[5] This coast-to-coast railroad, when it was built, was certain to bring economic prosperity to the areas it crossed.

Still hoping to outdo Butterfield, William Russell, a partner in the firm of Russell, Majors & Waddell, told government officials that his company could provide a daily stagecoach service through the central route if it were given a $900,000-a-year contract. A bill supporting this plan was presented to Congress but was blocked by senators from the South. These senators argued that the northern Rockies and Sierra Nevada mountain ranges in the West could often be impassable by stagecoach in the winter.[6]

Even though the Butterfield route took a longer path than some thought was necessary, people were still excited at the news of the Butterfield Express, also known as the Overland Mail. It sped communication between the eastern states and California by at least a week over any service that was currently in operation. It took Butterfield's company nearly a year to map out roads, build stations where livestock could be kept, buy animals and equipment, and hire the men who would be needed to operate this new service.

The Mail Arrives

When the first Butterfield Express coach carrying mail from San Francisco arrived in St. Louis, Missouri, on October 9, 1858, it was cause for celebration. People lined the streets, bands played, and a parade escorted the mail to the St. Louis post office.

A writer described the event:

> One of the most important events since the conquest of our Pacific empire [since white Americans gained control of the Far West] was consummated on Saturday, the 9th of October. On that day the first mail overland from San Francisco reached St. Louis, Mo., having accomplished the distance in 23 days and 4 hours, or 1 day and 20 hours shorter than contract time! New York and California are now in direct communication with each other by a line of travel exempt from the dangers and annoyances of the sea; the time of passage has been shortened by at least a week.[7]

Huge celebrations were also held in San Francisco when the mail from the East reached the city. Parades were held. People from all over town came out to greet the stagecoach driver. The possibility of relatively fast communication with the eastern states was a cause for celebration.

Difficulties Along the Route

Butterfield's drivers did not have to deal with the challenge of getting their mail coaches through snow-bound mountain trails, as they would have if they used the central route. But the Ox Bow Route was not without its problems. Drivers who drove the mail wagons through some parts of the Butterfield route had to deal with unfriendly American Indian tribes who lived in the region. Apache, Comanche, and Kiowa did not want whites to trespass on their territory. They often made life difficult for stagecoach drivers who dared to cross through tribal lands.

Besides that, the Butterfield route crossed some of the most dangerous desert regions of North America. The temperature became very hot in the summer. Water and food for the livestock were hard to find.

Even with the improvements in mail service that came with the Butterfield route, the problem of establishing a dependable service to the West was not completely solved. The Butterfield line had only enough room in its coaches to transport about a tenth of the mail going between the East and the West. The rest was taken by slow-moving wagons or steamships.

Transporting this relatively small amount of mail across the nation was very expensive for the United States government. Butterfield received $600,000 a year for running two mail coaches east and west every week. But the United States Postal Service only made about $27,000 a year for postage on the letters Butterfield transported.

The Push for a Transcontinental Railroad

Many people believed that building a railroad across the nation was the only real solution. In 1859, Postmaster Joseph Holt said,

Because of the convenience they had provided for the East, many people pushed for expanding railroads to the newly settled West. The dream of a transcontinental railroad would take many years to realize.

Until a railroad shall have been constructed across the continent, the conveyance [transportation] of the Pacific mail overland must be regarded as wholly impractical. . . . The $600,000 paid annually for carrying a few sacks of letters from the Mississippi to San Francisco via El Paso, through a waste and uninhabited country, would defray the aggregate cost [cover the total price] of mail transportation . . . in the states of Kentucky, Tennessee and North Carolina.[8]

Horace Greeley, the well-known editor of the *New York Tribune*, agreed. Not only would a transcontinental railroad improve mail service to California, but it would provide eastern businesses with an affordable way to sell their products in the West. After taking a trip through the West in 1859, Greeley wrote,

I believe that twenty million dollars of costly or perishable merchandise would annually seek California overland if there were a continuous line of railway from the Atlantic to the Pacific seaboard; and that this amount would steadily and rapidly increase. . . .

The Post-Office Department is now paying at least one million and a quarter for the conveyance of mails between the Atlantic and Gulf states and California, and was recently paying one million and a half. For this, it gets a semi-monthly mail by way of the Isthmus [of Panama] (six thousand miles, or more than double the distance direct), and a semi-weekly mail by the Butterfield route . . . which carries letters only.[9]

But Congress was so split by tensions between the North and the South that it could not decide on a route or agree on any bill that provided funds for building a transcontinental railroad. Congress would continue to vote down similar proposals for nearly ten years.

Demands for Faster Mail Service

Meanwhile, many people in California were becoming angry at the United States government for ordering the mail to be carried over the Ox Bow Route. The *San Francisco Bulletin* wrote,

> The energy and enterprise which have brought us the mails overland from St. Louis to San Francisco in from 18 to 24 days, if expended [used] upon as short and available route as can be found, would give us the mails regularly in sixteen days. It was a stupid blunder . . . which compelled the contractors to take the circuitous [indirect] route. . . .[10]

While government officials and businessmen were debating the merits of building a railroad to the West, California Senator William Gwin was working on an alternative plan. He hoped that a private contractor could be found who would take on the challenge of providing a faster mail service to the West without a government contract.

In 1860, Senator Gwin's dream was about to come true. William Russell, a businessman with years of experience transporting military goods and other freight to the West, was about to take on the challenge. When he met with Gwin, plans were made that marked a turning point in the development of rapid communication between the East and the West.

No one is certain who came up with the idea for the Pony Express. Some say it was William Russell, the owner of one of the largest transportation companies in America. Others give Senator Gwin the credit. Still others say that one of Russell's employees and Gwin discussed the idea years before the Pony Express actually went into service.

THE PONY EXPRESS IS ESTABLISHED

In any case, William H. Russell was the man who put the idea into action. He was the only person willing to risk his money and the reputation of his company on the belief that mail to the west could be delivered much faster and cheaper on the Central Route than on Butterfield's Ox Bow Route.

Transportation Hub of the West

During the mid-1800s, Leavenworth, Kansas, was a major hub of transportation. People who wanted to travel west beyond the Missouri River went there to buy wagons, food, livestock, and other supplies before they made their journey. By then, people were going west for many reasons. While some still hoped to find gold, many others moved because the price of land was much cheaper than in the East. Still others went west to start businesses, build churches, or to be with family members who had already settled there.

At times, wagon trains stretched from Leavenworth to the horizon. In 1860, a traveler reported that he passed nearly two thousand freight wagons on a three-hundred-fifty-mile trip between Denver, Colorado, and Fort Kearney in the Kansas Territory.[1] One visitor described the scene in Leavenworth:

> huge freight wagons on every street, at every corner. . . . There is heard the lumbering of these "prairie schooners," the bellowing of oxen, braying of mules, cracking of long lariats (whips) . . . the hollowing—yelling—of teamsters, mingled with more oaths than I ever heard before in all my life together.[2]

William H. Russell, Alexander Majors, and William B. Waddell had years of experience hauling cargo and passengers across the West. During the California gold rush, Russell and his business partners had made a fortune in the stagecoach and shipping business.

By 1858, Russell, Majors & Waddell had nearly monopolized the freight transportation business on the plains. They owned 6,250 wagons and 75,000 oxen.[3] Besides transporting supplies for ordinary citizens, Russell, Majors & Waddell had contracts to transport millions of pounds of food and supplies to army bases in the West.

At the time the Pony Express service was proposed, Russell, Majors & Waddell's express and transportation service was among the largest in the nation. In 1859, Horace Greeley described the company's headquarters in Leavenworth, Kansas: "Russell, Majors & Waddell's transportation establishment . . . is the great feature of Leavenworth. Such acres of wagons! . . . such herds of oxen! such regiments of drivers and other employees!"[4]

Russell, Majors & Waddell also had experience in carrying out government mail contracts. The firm already operated a successful mail and passenger coach service between the Missouri River and Salt Lake City.

William Russell believed that, if he set up a relay system of horse riders across the West, where riders would carry the mail both day and night, letters could be transported from Missouri to California in ten days or less. This would be under half the time required by mail coaches on Butterfield's Ox Bow Route.

Mail Delivery by Horse

The idea of using relay horse riders to carry the mail across vast distances had been around for many centuries. Rulers in Europe and the Orient often used swift horsemen to deliver messages. In the 1300s, Chinese ruler Genghis Khan used a relay system of thousands of riders to send messages to the far reaches of his kingdom.

From America's colonial years, horse riders were often used to transport important messages. In 1825, the postmaster general expanded on this idea. He hired men to carry mail on horseback between large cities in the East. The riders stopped to change horses every twelve to fifteen miles. This new service cut the delivery time on a letter from New York to New Orleans from sixteen days to seven days. But to limit the size of loads carried by express riders, postage costs were three times that of a letter transported by stagecoach.

This system generally worked well for transporting mail in the heavily populated regions of the East and Midwest. People were pleased to know that, if they had an urgent letter to send, they could expect it to be delivered as quickly as possible.

However, Americans who lived in the West still had to deal with slow and unreliable mail service. This was something William Russell hoped to change with his new service.

William Russell—Risk Taker

Russell had another reason for wanting to establish a Pony Express service to the West. He thought the publicity generated by this new service would improve his existing express and transportation business and attract new clients.

He knew that starting such a venture would be an expensive publicity stunt. But Russell felt sure that, once the service proved itself, he would have no trouble winning the congressional support necessary to secure a government contract. Then he would be able to make a fortune transporting the regular mail over the Central Overland Route by horse-drawn wagons.

Russell quickly saw an opportunity. And he was not afraid to take risks. Historian Ralph Moody said,

> Although his formal education was slight, his appearance, speech, and bearing were those of a cultured gentleman. He had a brilliant mind in many respects and considerable personal charm, and was animated by infinite confidence in his own judgment and ability. He was, however, extremely impulsive . . . [and] an extremely dangerous business associate.[5]

Conflict Within the Company

Starting a Pony Express service to transport mail to the West without a government contract was a very expensive and risky business venture. No one else had dared to attempt it. But Russell believed that the government mail contract he could win would make the Pony Express a good investment in the long run.[6]

His business partners, Majors and Waddell, however, were not so sure. They feared the company would have to commit more money to the

William Russell was the man who spearheaded the launch of the Pony Express.

venture than it would ever see in profits. And there was no way to be certain who might win a mail contract from the government. Alexander Majors said,

> Mr. Russell strenuously insisted that we stand by him, as he had committed himself to Senator Gwin before leaving Washington, assuring him that he could get his partners to join him, and that he might rely on the project being carried through, and saying it would be very humiliating to his pride to return to Washington and be compelled to say that the scheme had fallen through for lack of his partners' confidence.[7]

So even though they did not fully support the idea, Majors and Waddell reluctantly agreed to the venture.

Preparing for the Venture

Russell promised Senator Gwin that his company would be ready to begin mail service on the Central Route by April 1860. That gave them only sixty-seven days to put his plan into effect. It was not much time to buy horses, build station houses, and hire men. But Russell believed that with faith, hard work, and determination, anything could be accomplished.

Russell traveled to New York, Washington, D.C., and other large cities in the East to raise money for the venture. While he was in Washington, he made as many contacts as possible. He tried to gain the political support necessary for winning a government mail contract to the West.

While Russell was busy with the financial and political affairs of the business, William Waddell ran the home office. In many ways, Waddell and Russell were opposites. While Russell often involved himself in risky ventures, Waddell was known as a penny-pincher who often debated over business matters for a long time before coming to a decision.[8]

Alexander Majors, who was also much more conservative than Russell in business ventures, was put in charge of managing the details of the Pony Express's day-to-day operations. One of his responsibilities was to organize the mail route in the most efficient way possible.

Planning the Route

After studying a map, Majors decided to divide the route into five sections. Each section was three hundred to four hundred miles long. The first section of the Pony Express route ran from St. Joseph, Missouri, to Fort Kearny, in present-day Nebraska, on the Platte River. The second leg went from Fort Kearny to Horseshoe Station near Fort Laramie, Wyoming. These two sections followed the route of the Oregon-California Trail, and dipped into present-day Colorado at Julesburg.

The third section of the Pony Express route took the same trail that early western travelers had used to travel from Fort Bridger, Wyoming, to the Salt Lake Valley in Utah. The fourth section went through the Great Basin area of Utah and Nevada. This was south of the California Trail, along the Humbolt River. Army explorers opened this trail, which was used by Mormon settlers when they traveled to western Utah

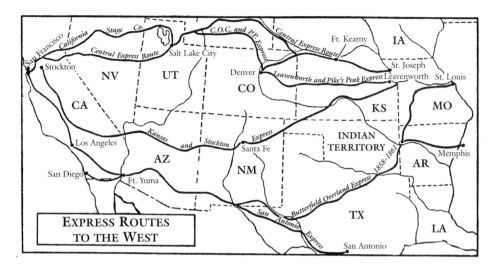

This map shows the various routes most often used to get to the West in the nineteenth century, including the Butterfield Route and the Central Express, or Overland, Route, which was used by the Pony Express.

to escape religious persecution in the East. It went south of the Great Salt Lake Desert to Roberts Creek Station, north of Eureka, Nevada. This part of the route became present-day United States Highway 50.

The final leg of the route, which crossed Nevada's Great Basin desert and passed through the mountains of the Sierra Nevada, just south of Lake Tahoe, was thought to be the toughest leg of the trip.[9] It was especially treacherous during the winter months, when heavy snow made traveling through the mountains extremely difficult.

Station Houses

Since Russell, Majors & Waddell had been transporting freight to the West for years, it already owned many buildings along the trail. But to provide for the requirements of a speedy Pony Express service, where riders could change horses every ten to fifteen miles, many additional buildings had to be built.

According to Russell's plan, home stations were built at intervals of seventy-five to one hundred miles apart. Home stations gave riders a place to eat, sleep, and relax between their runs. Relay stations, where riders could change horses, have a bite to eat, or get emergency supplies, were to be built every ten to fifteen miles. Relay stations were usually much smaller than home stations. Because of the limited time to prepare, only eighty-six stations had been completed when the service began its first run. On average, these stations were twenty to twenty-five miles apart.

Russell, Majors & Waddell also had to provide all the stations with supplies. Even the smallest relay station required a constant supply of food, both for people and for livestock. Home stations had even more requirements. Some home stations had blacksmith shops where horseshoes could be made.

Before the mail service could start, huge supplies of ham, flour, bacon, coffee, tea, sugar, cornmeal, dried fruit, and other foods had to be bought and transported west. Other necessities for relay and home stations included blankets, pans and dishes, and candles.

The stations also had to be supplied with tools, spare parts, equipment for horses, and other items Pony Express riders and station hands needed frequently.

This Pony Express station was located along the route at Cheese Creek, Nebraska.

These included horse combs and brushes, nails for horseshoes, bridles, and rope.

Pony Express stations in the desert regions of the West had special needs. Water often had to be carried in by wagon. If grass was scarce, horses sometimes had to be driven miles away from the station house to an area where they could find enough to eat.

Advertising for Horses

In January 1860, newspapers announced that plans were in the works to establish a horse express mail service to California. A few weeks later, this story was confirmed. Russell and his partners placed advertisements for horses in newspapers across the West.

The Pony Express set out to buy the best horses available. And the owners were willing to pay top dollar. Majors knew that having a fast horse could mean the difference between riders successfully transporting the mail across the West and being killed by bandits or American Indians.

Advertising for Riders and Station Hands

Another important task was advertising for riders and station hands. Russell, Majors & Waddell had to find men and boys who were able to ride up to one hundred miles a day. They must also be able to deal with harsh weather and road conditions. In some parts of the route, they had to be ready to deal with attacks from American Indians.

Russell, Majors & Waddell decided to pay Pony Express riders $100 to $120 a month, plus room and board. A few riders who would cover more miles than average or were assigned to travel through particularly dangerous territory were paid up to $150. At the time, that was much more than most people could earn by riding horses for a living. The firm knew that high pay would attract the best riders available.

The company preferred to hire orphans. They did not want to deal with grieving parents if riders were attacked and killed. Hundreds of boys and young men replied. Despite all the danger involved, many were excited to play a part in such an important undertaking.

Riders selected for the Pony Express could not weigh more than 120 pounds. Most riders who qualified were younger than twenty years old and weighed under one hundred pounds. Many Pony Express riders were similar in size to modern-day jockeys. Their small size made it possible for the horses to run as fast as possible.

The Pony Express also needed division superintendents to oversee the routes and make sure everything ran as smoothly as possible. Russell, Majors & Waddell offered $90 per month plus room and board to men who qualified for that position. Station keepers, whose duties included taking care of the horses and supervising the station houses, were paid from $50 to $100 per month.

Riding Equipment

Before the Pony Express service could begin, a wide variety of equipment had to be purchased for horses and

---

SOURCE DOCUMENT

THE RIDERS ARE MOSTLY YOUTHS, MOUNTED UPON ACTIVE AND LITHE INDIAN NAGS [HORSES]. THEY RIDE 100 MILES AT A TIME—ABOUT EIGHT PER HOUR—WITH FOUR CHANGES OF HORSES, AND RETURN TO THEIR STATION THE NEXT DAY: OF THEIR HARDSHIPS AND PERILS WE SHALL HEAR MORE ANON. THE LETTERS ARE CARRIED IN LEATHER BAGS, WHICH ARE THROWN ABOUT CARELESSLY ENOUGH WHEN THE SADDLE IS CHANGED, AND THE AVERAGE POSTAGE IS $5 . . . PER SHEET. [10]

British explorer, writer, and world traveler Sir Richard Francis Burton described Pony Express riders.

riders. Almost as soon as the decision to start the service was made, Russell, Majors & Waddell placed rush orders for saddles, horseshoes, and other riding equipment.

After considering his options, Russell decided that the best way for riders to carry the mail was in a lightweight saddlebag, known as a *mochila*. The mochila had four leather pouches in which mail was carried. Each pouch had a brass padlock to ensure that no one could remove the letters between stations. Only the station masters had a key. To protect it from the rain, mail was wrapped in oiled cloth before it was locked into the mochila. The mochila fit over the rider's saddle horn and could quickly be changed from one horse to another.

Hiring Riders

By the time the Pony Express service started, eighty young men had been hired as mail riders. At the insistence of Alexander Majors, who was known to be very religious, each young man who was hired to ride for the new Pony Express mail service was required to take the following oath:

> While I am in the employ of A. Majors, I agree not to use profane language, not to get drunk, not to gamble, not to treat animals cruelly, and not to do anything else that is incompatible with the conduct of a gentleman. And I agree, if I violate any of the above conditions, to accept my discharge without any pay for my services.[11]

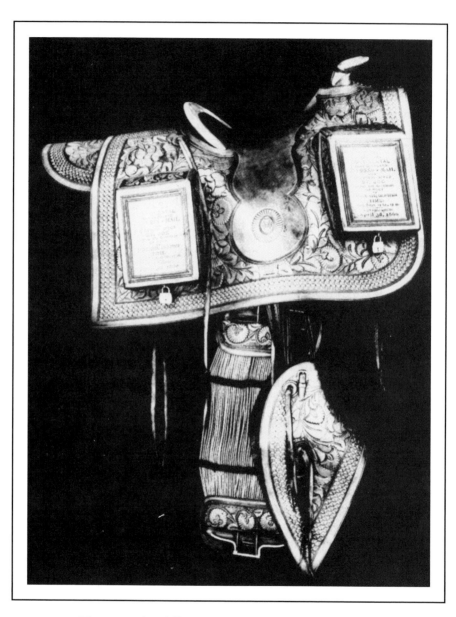

This type of saddle was used by Pony Express riders.

After the riders took the oath, they were presented with a Bible, which Majors also believed would help prevent poor behavior. Majors believed that requiring riders to take this oath would weed out employees who were likely to cause trouble.

Pony Express riders were issued two Colt revolvers and a rifle. But even with these weapons, riders had to be careful as they crossed through remote regions of the West. The company warned riders not to start trouble with American Indians or western bandits. If a dispute did start, they were instructed never to be the first to fire their weapon. Pony Express riders had fast horses that could outrun nearly any animal in the West. Fleeing from trouble, the riders were told, was always their best option.

The Excitement Builds

The Pony Express created quite a stir across the nation. This was especially true among the people in St. Joseph, Missouri, where the route started, and in San Francisco, California, and other parts of the West. Western miners and settlers were eager to see if this new service would really deliver the mail as quickly as it promised.

But despite all the excitement over the new mail route to California, some people had their doubts. Many feared that American Indian tribes in the West would ambush and kill the young Pony Express riders before they could reach California with the mail.

Would it really be possible for an express service to deliver mail reliably from Missouri to California in a week? Or would the plan fail, as some predicted? As the firm of Russell, Majors & Waddell made the final preparations for the first run of the Pony Express, the entire nation watched in anticipation.

5

THE FIRST RIDE OF THE PONY EXPRESS

On April 3, 1860, the Pony Express began its first run. In St. Joseph, Missouri, hundreds of people turned out to see the rider off. Many people showed their support by displaying American flags or hanging brightly colored ribbons from their homes and businesses.

The riders were given free rooms at Patee House, the Pony Express headquarters in St. Joseph. During the days before the first run, riders frequently attended Patee House dances, sporting the colorful shirts and blue jeans they would wear on the job. But now the dancing was over. The mail riders knew it was time to turn their attention to the serious job of delivering messages over the vast, untamed regions of the West.

St. Joseph Sends Off the First Pony Express Rider

The people of St. Joseph, Missouri, could hardly contain their enthusiasm for Russell, Majors & Waddell's new venture. By mid-afternoon, a large group of men, women, and children had gathered around Patee

House, where they waited for the horse and rider to appear.

Many important people made speeches about the Pony Express and what the new mail delivery service meant to St. Joseph and the nation. A brass band was there to entertain the crowd until the mail to be sent west arrived.

M. Jeff Thompson, the mayor of St. Joseph, was the first to step up to the podium. Thompson talked about "the significance of the Express to our city over the Central Overland Route."[1] He said,

> This is a great day in the history of St. Joseph. . . . For the first time in [the] history of America, mail will go by an overland route from East to West. It is the hope of this community that this enterprise is but the forerunner of a day which will see not only the extension of the telegraph clear to California, but also the time when steam will drive a railroad train through those vastnesses and bear passengers from St. Joseph to California in less than a week![2]

The crowd cheered wildly when a "bright bay mare" was led out.[3] The first run of the Pony Express was about to begin.

The *Missouri* Brings the Mail to St. Joseph

While politicians made speeches to the eager crowd, another remarkable accomplishment in transportation was taking place. In 1860, St. Joseph received most mail from the East by steamboat. The United States government had not yet signed any mail contracts with railroad lines. But the owners of the Hannibal and St.

Joseph Railroad wanted to show the government what a train was capable of doing. So they took on the job of delivering the first load of mail from the East to the Pony Express.

A wood-powered train engine, named the *Missouri*, was specially selected for the job. The railroad's owners wanted to do everything possible to make sure nothing went wrong and that the *Missouri* made the trip from Hannibal, Missouri, to St. Joseph, Missouri, as quickly as possible. An article published in the *New York Sun* said,

> Every man on the line considered himself an important part of the event. George H. Davis, the roadmaster, issued orders for every switch to be spiked [set to go as quickly as possible] and all trains kept off the main line. He was selected to make the run, with a nervy engineer, "Ad" Clark at the throttle. . . . The orders given to Engineer Clark were simple. He was to make a speed record to stand for fifty years.[4]

Clark accomplished his goal. He drove the *Missouri* 206 miles in only 4 hours and 51 minutes.[5] It was a record that would stand for many years to come.

A little after 7:00 P.M., the *Missouri* blew its whistle as it pulled into St. Joseph. The crowd immediately burst into excited cheers. They knew the moment they had been waiting for had finally come.

A special messenger brought a bag of mail from the train and turned it over to a Pony Express official. In addition to letters and telegrams, the bag contained a few copies of the *St. Joseph Gazette,* the *New York Herald*, and the *New York Tribune.* These newspapers were printed on extremely thin paper to make them as light as possible. The mail was wrapped in oiled silk to protect it from rain, locked into the mochila, and placed over the saddle of the horse.

The rider wore a red shirt, blue pants, riding gloves, and boots. The horse's saddle and bridle were decorated with fancy silver embroidery. While there is still some debate, most historians believe that the first Pony Express rider to leave St. Joseph was Johnny Fry.

The Rider Is Off!

At 7:25 P.M., the ceremony was finally over. Fry was ready to leave. The crowd cheered as Fry and his horse boarded the ferry that would take him across the Missouri River. A cannon was fired in front of the Patee House to signal the ferryboat operator to be on the Missouri side of the Missouri River.

During the ride across the river, Fry took off his fancy outfit and put on more comfortable work clothes. The ferry docked in Elwood, Kansas. There, Fry was greeted by a smaller crowd of well-wishers.

Fry passed through Elwood and rode on to the West. He passed through a region where the Kickapoo lived, a tribe that lived mostly by farming and was friendly toward white settlers. After traveling nearly a hundred miles and changing horses several times, he reached his home station in Marysville, Kansas. Fry then turned the mail over to the next rider and enjoyed a good meal and a night of well-earned rest.

Johnny Fry is widely believed to have been the first rider to carry the mail westward from St. Joseph, Missouri, on the Pony Express.

The Mail

The Pony Express charged five dollars per half-ounce of mail for delivering letters. That would be equivalent to more than eighty dollars in today's money. Because of the extremely high cost of postage, few people could actually afford the service. As a result, only a few dozen letters and a small number of telegrams and newspapers were sent west on the first run of the Pony Express.

By the spring of 1860, telegraph wires had already been strung between New York City and St. Joseph, Missouri. So telegraph messages received at the St. Joseph office could quickly be printed and sent to California by way of the Pony Express. This sped the delivery of messages from New York to the West by several days.

The First Pony Express Rider Leaves San Francisco

On that same day, as the first westbound Pony Express rider left St. Joseph, Missouri, the city of San Francisco, California, held a huge celebration to send off its first eastbound Pony Express rider. The first rider was scheduled to leave from the *Alta Telegraph* newspaper's office on Montgomery Street at 4:00 P.M. on April 3. The *Alta California*, another San Francisco newspaper, invited its readers to give the "Horse Express," a good "send-off."[6] San Francisco's population was happy to comply with the newspaper's request.

The next day, the *Alta Telegraph* wrote,

The first Pony Express started yesterday afternoon. . . . The saddle bags were duly lettered "Overland Pony Express," and the horse (a wiry little animal) was dressed with miniature flags. He proceeded, just before four o'clock, to the Sacramento boat, and was cheered on by the crowd as he started. . . . The express matter amounted to 85 letters, which at $5 per letter gave a total receipt of $425.[7]

Although few people knew it, the rider they celebrated did not really work for the Pony Express. James Randall, who sat in for the occasion, had to take the mail and horse only to the San Francisco waterfront, and put them on board a steamboat called the *Antelope*, bound for Sacramento, California. That is where the real ride would begin.

At approximately 2:00 A.M. on April 4, the *Antelope* docked at Sacramento. Because of the late hour, the Sacramento docks were quiet. There were no crowds to cheer the rider on or to celebrate the historic occasion. Many historians believe that Sam Hamilton was the first Pony Express rider to carry the eastbound mail. But other possible riders were also mentioned in magazines and newspapers of the time. Hamilton picked up a few letters going east and started his ride to Sportsman's Hall, a Pony Express station about sixty miles east of Sacramento.

Problems With Bad Weather

Everyone knew that severe weather might cause problems and delays. From the beginning, Pony Express riders had to deal with an unusual amount of rain, snow, and cold weather.

Sam Hamilton started his route in pouring rain. As he rode into the foothills of the Sierra Nevada mountains, the rain changed to snow. When "Boston" Upson started the next leg of the mail route, the weather was even worse. Historian Ralph Moody wrote,

> Above the four-thousand-foot level a raging blizzard was blowing, and gales at more than sixty miles an hour piled snow fifteen to twenty feet deep. The trail was completely obliterated [covered], and visibility reduced to less than a hundred feet, but Boston fought his way upwards from one isolated relay post to another.[8]

Upson transported the mail to Friday's Station, on the California-Nevada border.

On April 8, eastbound and westbound Pony Express riders passed each other near the present-day town of Farson, Wyoming. Despite the bad weather, Pony Express riders knew the importance of their job. So they continued to move the mail from station to station.

Pony Express riders normally rode one hundred miles a day. They changed horses seven to twelve times during a day's ride. They averaged a speed of eight miles per hour, but under ideal conditions, riders were sometimes able to make ten miles per hour.[9] Once they had completed their run, a new rider would take the mochila on to the next station.

The Mail Reaches Its Destination

A huge reception was waiting for the Pony Express rider to bring mail from the East into Sacramento. When he galloped into San Francisco at about 1:00 A.M. on April 14, cannon fire and a mounted escort of men on horseback greeted him.

After delivering mail to Sacramento, the rider galloped aboard the steamship *Antelope* to be taken down to San Francisco by river. When he arrived, another large, noisy celebration awaited him. Nearly two thousand people came to watch the steamboat land with the Pony Express rider bringing mail from the East. Cheering citizens lined the streets. Banners and bells greeted riders along the way into town. A band played "See the Conquering Hero Comes." San Francisco's celebration of the first mail delivery by Pony Express continued long into the night.

Because of Russell's bold plan for a Pony Express service, Californians and other settlers in the West were no longer as isolated as they had been in the past. With dependable mail service to keep them informed of happenings in the East, for the first time, they truly felt connected to the rest of the nation.

6

THE LIVES OF PONY EXPRESS RIDERS

While the Pony Express was in operation, the riders' lives were glamorized in stories, songs, articles, and poems. Many young boys dreamed that they would someday have the chance to ride across the West for Russell's company. The riders who took the mail across the country were seen as heroes—men who performed a service that was vital to the nation.

But in reality, the lives of Pony Express riders were anything but glamorous. Their lives were difficult and dangerous. Writer Mark Twain made it clear that the men who rode for the Pony Express had to be ready to face nearly any situation. Twain wrote,

> No matter what time of the day or night his watch came on, and no matter whether it was winter or summer, raining, snowing, hailing, or sleeting, or whether his "beat" was a level straight road or a crazy trail over mountain crags and precipices, or whether it led through peaceful regions or regions that swarmed with hostile Indians, he must always be ready to leap into the saddle and be off like the wind![1]

Dangers on the Trail

When a Pony Express rider started each mail ride, he had no idea what awaited him. Sometimes, the weather was perfect and he had no problems at all. Other times, he had to push through blizzards and guide his horse through narrow mountain passes in the blinding snow. Winter weather made it especially difficult for riders who had to take their horses through the Sierra Nevada mountains. Sometimes, the snow was so deep that the horse could barely get through.

Roads that were used to haul freight through mountain passes to mines in Nevada were kept open most of the winter. But snow was still a problem in other areas. Deep snow often covered the high mountain passes between Salt Lake City, Utah, and Fort Laramie, Wyoming. But despite the deep winter snow, Pony Express customers seldom had to wait more than several days beyond the scheduled time for the mail to arrive.

Summer weather also posed a problem for Pony Express riders, especially those who had to cross desert regions. Water was scarce, and the trail to the next station house could sometimes be hard to follow. If a rider and his horse became lost, they could quickly die of thirst. On other parts of the route, fast-moving summer storms often flooded paths that Express riders could normally cross.

Besides dealing with extreme weather conditions, Express riders constantly had to be on guard against attacks. They had to watch out for bandits who lived

SOURCE DOCUMENT

I TOLD HIM I COULD RIDE FAST AND STAND UP UNDER [HARD?] GOING, COULD SHOOT FAST AND STRAIGHT AND DID NOT THINK I WAS YELLOW. IT WAS NECESSARY TO GIVE A $1000 BOND BEFORE I COULD GO TO WORK. [BUFFALO BILL] CODY RECOMMENDED ME AND WENT ON MY BOND. THAT STARTED ME ON A . . . SPELL AS A RIDER FOR THE PONY EXPRESS. MY TRAIL WAS BETWEEN FORT DODGE AND WICHITA KANS[AS]. THE PONY EXPRESS CARRIED REGISTERED MAIL AND THERE WAS CONSIDERABLE VALUABLE MONEY IN OUR CARE. IT WAS THE FAST METHOD OF THAT DAY, LIKE THE AIRPLANE IS TODAY.[2]

A former Pony Express rider gave this account of his experience many years later.

in the desert. Many outlaws who were not welcome in western towns roamed the plains. And a lone rider always made a good target.

Other hazards also awaited Pony Express riders. Historian Will Bagley wrote,

> Carrying the mail was a dangerous job and some five riders died along the trail. Newspapers reported that in April 1860, a rider was killed when his horse "stumbled over an ox lying in the road." While crossing the Platte River the next July, a courier was thrown from his horse [and was killed]. . . . A young German got lost near Fort Kearny in December and froze to death. Newspapers reported that several riders were killed during the Paiute War [in Nevada], and William Fisher recalled the Indians killed "four of our brave riders."[3]

Even under the best conditions, being a Pony Express rider was not an easy job. A rider had to spend many hours alone in the saddle, pushing his horse to make the best possible speed to the next station. Even though the riders knew the importance of their job, it was difficult to go for months without seeing friends and family back home. In isolated regions of the West, the only people Pony Express riders saw for months were station hands and other riders.

Because of the hardships and dangers, some Pony Express riders did not stay on the job for long. But for every rider who quit, many other young riders were willing to take his place. In the beginning, eighty riders were hired to carry the mail. But even at the service's peak, there were never more than one hundred twenty riders working for the Pony Express at any one time.

Despite the bad weather and other problems they encountered, Pony Express riders nearly always accomplished what they set out to do—deliver mail from Missouri to California in ten days or less.

Carrying the Mail

Pony Express riders were expected to be able carry up to twenty pounds of mail. Often, the amount of mail was much less than twenty pounds, but that was the top limit. They also carried up to twenty-five pounds of supplies, including guns, the mochila, the saddle, and other riding equipment. Because it was important to keep their load as light as possible, most Pony

Frank E. Webner was one of the many young riders who took bold chances riding for the Pony Express.

Express riders eventually decided to carry only a Colt pistol or no firearms at all.

Author Henry T. Williams described the riders:

> An express messenger left once a week from each side with not more than ten pounds of matter [an average load]. The best riders were chosen from among trappers, scouts and plains men, familiar with all the life of the route, fearless, and capable of great physical power, endurance and bravery. The ponies were very swift and strong, a cross between the American horse and Indian pony, and after each run of sixty miles, waited till the arrival of the messenger from the opposite direction. . . .[4]

A few months after the Pony Express was in operation, Russell, Majors & Waddell decided to improve the service by providing mail delivery twice a week. This change went into effect on June 10, 1860.[5]

Pony Express Stations

A Pony Express station out on the horizon was always a welcome sight to riders. As soon as the station master heard a mail rider coming, he jumped into action. He got a fresh horse ready and prepared to help the rider change the mochila to the new saddle. Pony Express riders were expected to change horses and be on their way to the next station in two minutes or less. But unless they were behind schedule, riders often took breaks between runs. They used this time to eat, drink, or walk around the station house before starting the next leg of the journey.

On the eastern and western ends of the route, most home station houses were built out of wood. Those in Utah and Nevada were made mostly of adobe bricks. These bricks were made from clay that was readily available in the area. Many stations were built of stone, and the foundations remain today. In the central section of the route, some station houses were made of sod. Many station houses were built from a combination of these materials. In some areas, where wood was scarce, some stations lacked roofs.

Station houses served as a home not only to the station hands who lived there and took care of the horses, but to riders who spent their days rushing loads of mail between the stations. This is where they ate, slept, visited with friends who worked for the Express, and kept whatever personal belongings they wanted to have with them on the trail. While some stations were very modest and isolated, others were large and close to towns.

Relay stations had many of the same supplies and equipment as home stations. However, their primary function was to provide a place for Pony Express riders to exchange horses. Like the home stations, relay stations were built out of whatever materials were available. While most were made of wood, stone, or adobe bricks, a few Pony Express relay stations were even built in holes or caverns in a hill or mountain. They were usually protected with logs, brush, and a sod roof. One writer described a Pony Express relay station at Dugway, Utah, as "A hole, four feet deep, roofed over with split cedar trunks and with a rough adobe chimney. Water had to be brought in casks."[6]

All home and relay stations had a corral and stalls where horses could be kept. The fences were made of logs, stones, or whatever material was handy. Mules used for Russell, Majors & Waddell's other transportation businesses were often kept in these corrals. Some Pony Express stations were used as depots for stagecoach passengers, especially west of Salt Lake City, Utah.

Approximately once a month, Russell, Majors & Waddell sent wagon trains from the East to bring fresh supplies to the Express stations. It was always a big day for station employees when they opened the packages to see the food, medicine, and provisions that would take them through the next thirty days.

The Reality of Frontier Life

Life on the frontier was rough. In many parts of the West, there was little, if any, law enforcement. Majors had required all Pony Express employees to take an oath not to drink alcoholic beverages, use profane language, or gamble before they were hired. Some took this oath very seriously. However, many riders saw the oath only as a formality. Alcoholic drinks were available throughout much of the West. Some station houses were built within walking distance of bars. The temptation to break the oath was often more than Pony Express riders and station hands could resist.

The Paiute War

When the Pony Express service started, most American Indians who lived along the western mail route were at peace with white settlers. Occasionally, small groups of Indians made raids on stations, but it was not a serious problem. However, soon after the Pony Express service started, a full-scale war between white settlers and the Paiute tribe broke out.

The conflict was caused by problems that had been building for years between white miners and the Paiute. White trappers and traders first came to the present-day state of Nevada in the 1830s. The American Indians there were on good terms with most of these men. The whites usually left after they had taken care of their business, and they were not numerous enough to cause problems. Then, in the 1840s, Mormon settlers came to Utah. At first, some tribes were concerned. Never had so many white settlers entered their land and stayed there. But the Indians soon learned that the Mormons wanted to live in peace.

But the men who went west during the California gold rush were different. They did not care about living in peace with the Indian tribes. If a conflict arose, many white settlers would not hesitate to kill Indians. American Indians were often killed for no reason other than sport. In some parts of the West, white miners used American Indians as slaves and forced them to pan for gold.

When gold was discovered in western Nevada in 1859, white settlers took over land that once belonged to the Paiute and other tribes. The American Indians often saw the whites killing game, cutting down fruit trees, and using other resources that had always belonged to the tribes. This went on for over a decade. But the tribes' complaints went unheeded. In the spring of 1860, Paiute tribes decided to fight back. Before the war was over, they had attacked nearly every white settlement in western Utah and eastern Nevada.

Pony Express stations in Nevada were a prime target for Paiute attacks. Because of the Paiute War, the Pony Express had to make many changes in its rides through Nevada. Sometimes, riders had to make double or triple runs because the station houses had been raided or destroyed.

Bob Tate was one Pony Express rider who found himself in the middle of the Paiute War. He put up a brave fight to defend the pouch of mail he carried. But before the day was over, Tate was killed in battle.

During the Paiute War, Robert "Pony Bob" Haslam made the longest ride in the history of the Pony Express. He picked up the eastbound mail (probably the May 10, 1860, mail from San Francisco) at Friday's Station. When he reached Buckland's Station, his relief rider was so frightened by the Indian threat that he refused to take the mail.

Pony Bob agreed to take the mail all the way to Smith's Creek without stopping to rest. That station was 115 miles away. When he got there, no rider was

The Paiute War took a heavy toll on the riders of the Pony Express, who were caught up in the violence between white settlers and the Paiute who, like this family, wanted to keep their land.

available. So Pony Bob had to carry the mail to yet another station. When he arrived, he saw that the station had been attacked by the Paiute and was in flames. When he came even closer, he saw that the station keeper had been killed.

So Pony Bob rode on to yet another station. This time, he found that the station house had not been raided. A rider was available to take the mail on the next leg of its journey. Haslam was then able to rest from his historic ride, which covered 190 miles in thirty-six hours.

After a rest of nine hours, Haslam retraced his route with the westbound mail. At Cold Springs, he found that Indians had raided the station. They had killed the station keeper and chased away all of the livestock. Finally, he reached Buckland's Station, making the 380-mile round trip, the longest on record.

Pony Express riders had one advantage over the Paiute. Their horses were usually stronger and faster than those of the tribes. Years before the Paiute War, the United States cavalry discovered that horses that ate a steady diet of grain, like those of the Pony Express, could outrun horses that ate only grass, like those of the Paiute. With this knowledge, as well as the strong horses Russell had bought for his Pony Express, the lives of many riders were saved.

The conflict with the Paiute tribe cost the lives of seventeen Pony Express employees. Most of the men who were killed had worked at station houses. In fact, the conflicts with the Paiute became so severe at one point that Pony Express service through the area had to be suspended from May 31 to June 26, 1860. The conflict with the Paiute seriously disrupted mail service to the West for several weeks. Some people began to wonder whether the Central Overland Route really were the best way to transport mail. Finally, the United States Army was brought in to settle the conflict, and the Pony Express was able to resume mail service.

Despite all the problems, Russell, Majors & Waddell's firm did a better job than anyone else in providing reliable mail service to the West. In November 1860, British explorer Sir Richard Francis Burton praised the service when he wrote,

> In . . . 1860, "the great dream of news transmitted from New York to San Francisco (more strictly speaking from St. Joseph to Placerville, California) in eight days was tested." It appeared, in fact, under the form of an advertisement in the St. Louis "Republican," and threw at once into the shade the great Butterfield Mail, whose expedition had been the theme of universal praise. . . .[7]

The Telegraph

While the Pony Express was trying its best to impress the public with feats of speed, a new and even faster method of communicating over long distances was being developed. Telegraph operators had been transmitting messages between cities in the eastern part of the nation since 1844. Now, a plan was under way to extend this service to the West. Sir Richard Francis Burton acknowledged this when he wrote,

At the moment of writing (Nov., 1860), the distance between New York and San Francisco has been farther reduced by the advance of the electric telegraph—it proceeds at the rate of six miles a day—to Fort Kearney from the Mississippi and to Fort Churchill from the Pacific side. The merchant thus receives his advances in six days.[8]

7

THE FINAL MONTHS OF THE PONY EXPRESS

Even though the Pony Express was successful in its mission to deliver mail to the West, the firm of Russell, Majors & Waddell was suffering great financial hardships. At the time that Russell, Majors & Waddell started the Pony Express, the firm was heavily financed by private loans. These loans were made against property the company owned and money the United States government owed the company. These loans made it possible for the company to continue its freight business and to establish the Pony Express.

In a letter to William Waddell during the summer of 1860, William Russell wrote, "I was compelled to build a world-wide reputation, even at considerable expense . . . and also to incur [become responsible for] large expenses in many ways, the details of which I cannot commit to paper."[1]

From the beginning, the Pony Express was operating at a loss. At one point, it had to take an average loss of thirteen dollars on every letter it delivered. During the summer of 1860, the Pony Express and Russell's other transport and freight businesses were losing up to $1,000 a day.

Hope for a Government Mail Contract

The future of Russell, Majors & Waddell depended on winning the government's overland mail contract. By the spring of 1860, the growing conflict between the Northern and Southern states was already starting to disrupt mail service in the Southern region of the Butterfield Ox Bow Route. This disruption in service gave Russell hopes of winning a contract to transport the mail on the Central Route. If he could win a mail contract to the West, Russell knew he could repay his loans and save his company.

On June 13, 1860, Russell's expectations were high. He sent a progress report to Waddell: "I am in treaty for tri-weekly mail at $600,000.00 which have hope of closing today. And although it will pay very handsome it is not as good as we wanted. It will however lay the foundation for a mail which will give us $1,200,000.00."[2]

But things did not turn out as Russell hoped. With the threat of a civil war brewing between the North and the South, Congress had other matters to consider. It adjourned without taking any action on the mail bill. Not one to give up easily, California Senator William Gwin urged President James Buchanan to appropriate $900,000 for Russell's plan to deliver mail west over the Central Overland Route. But Buchanan refused to act on the proposal. Gwin reminded Buchanan that, if Congress took no action, and public necessity required it, Buchanan had promised to authorize a mail contract over the Central Overland Route. Still, Buchanan refused to take action on the matter.[3]

One More Chance

Russell knew his company had to do something to prove to the nation that its service was better than any other method of communication. A national election was coming up in the fall of 1860. If the Pony Express could transport the news of who had been elected the next president to California before anyone else, it would once again prove the value of its service. Russell hoped this would impress Congress enough to consider giving his company a contract for delivery of the overland mail by stagecoach.

On November 7, 1860, Americans elected Abraham Lincoln to be their next president. As soon as the news from Washington, D.C., reached Fort Kearny, the most distant point to which news could be sent from the East by telegraph, Pony Express riders went into action. Their job was to carry the message eighteen hundred miles to Fort Churchill, Nevada, where a telegraph operator would be waiting to transmit the news to San Francisco.

On November 7, a Pony Express rider left the telegraph office at Fort Kearny. The snow was heavy on much of the route. Despite severe weather, the riders

The expansion of telegraph lines made it easier to relay important news from the Pony Express's headquarters in Missouri, but also threatened one day to put the Express out of business.

kept up their pace. In only three days and four hours, the news of Lincoln's election reached Salt Lake City, Utah. As soon as the Pony Express rider carrying the dispatch reached Fort Churchill, Nevada, the telegraph operator went to work. By November 17, San Francisco newspapers were able to print the story of Lincoln's election.

Lincoln's election gave hope to Californians who had come from the Northern states. Soon after hearing the news, the California state legislature passed a resolution pledging the state's support to the Union. The Pony Express had helped keep the nation together.

The Indian Bond Scandal

Publicity stunts, such as delivering the news of Lincoln's election to the West in record time, brought Russell, Majors & Waddell much fame. But they did not bring the government mail contract the firm had hoped for.

By the winter of 1860, Russell, Majors & Waddell was going broke. To obtain the money it needed to pay bills and keep the freight and mail services running, Russell went to New York to try to obtain new loans. But this was not as easy as Russell had hoped. Many bankers and private investors knew that Russell's businesses were financially shaky. They did not want to risk money on his ventures.

Russell was especially concerned because some loans that his friend, Secretary of War John B. Floyd, had signed would soon be due. If he did not have the money to pay them, it would cause serious problems for Floyd as well as for Russell's company.

Through his contacts in Washington, Russell met with Godard Baily, a minor official in the Interior Department. Baily had access to Indian Trust Bonds, which Russell could use as collateral to get more loans. Indian Trust Bonds were government bonds that were supposed to be used to help American Indian tribes. Baily was related to Floyd by marriage and did not want to see Floyd embarrassed or forced to resign his position. So he allowed Russell to borrow the bonds and use them to obtain more loans. His only request was that the bonds be returned to him within ninety days.

Russell immediately took the Indian Trust Bonds to New York. There, he used them to borrow enough money to cover his debt to Floyd. But his company was still in deep financial trouble. He went back to Washington that September and convinced Baily to loan him more bonds so he could repay his debts and keep the company running. This time, Baily loaned Russell $387,000 worth of bonds.

By then, the conflict between the North and the South had pushed the financial world into turmoil. The value of many stocks and bonds was quickly falling. Even with government-issued Indian Trust Bonds as collateral, Russell was not able to borrow as much money as he needed to pay a debt that grew larger every day.

Russell headed back to Washington that December to make one more request of Baily. If Baily loaned him $350,000 worth of Indian Trust Bonds, Russell promised, he could recover his losses and keep them all out of trouble. Baily did not want to do it. But Russell was desperate. He kept pleading for the bonds until Baily reluctantly agreed. Russell took the bonds and left.

After considering the matter for a few days, Baily realized it would be impossible for Russell to repay the money in time. On December 22, he decided to confess the entire scheme to his superiors before the loans came due.

Two days later, the scandal was exposed. Russell and Baily were arrested for embezzlement and jailed. Floyd was forced to resign from his position as secretary of war. Both Floyd and Baily eventually fled to the South.[4]

Russell claimed that he had accepted the bonds only to make certain that his wagons would run and continue to ship supplies the army needed in the West. A few days later, he was released from jail.

Russell voluntarily appeared before a congressional committee. On January 29, 1861, he, along with Floyd and Baily, was indicted for fraud because of the improper use of the Indian Bonds. But none of the men involved with the Indian Bond scandal was ever brought to trial.[5] In March 1861, the charges against Russell were dropped on a legal technicality. By then, however, the scandal had stained his reputation and nearly destroyed his company. But even after all that had happened, Russell had some powerful friends. He stayed in Washington for a while and tried to save what he could of his business empire.

Not everyone blamed Russell for what had happened. Some people felt that the Indian Bond scandal was a conspiracy to discredit Russell's firm and prevent him from getting the government mail contract—a set-up by Southerners who wanted a mail route through the South, or even by the United States government, which owed money to Russell, Majors & Waddell.[6]

Congress Approves the Central Route

As the conflict between the North and the South continued to tear the nation apart, Congress was forced once again to consider the issue of overland mail delivery. The United States government realized that something had to be done. On February 2, 1861, the annual Post Route Bill passed. It included an $800,000 appropriation for mail to be delivered by stagecoach on the Central Route six days a week. Then the debate over who should get the mail contract began.

With the Indian Bond scandal still fresh in the minds of many Americans, a bid from Russell, Majors & Waddell could not be approved. Instead, the contract went to the company Butterfield had started, the Overland Mail Company.

One congressman declared that the service provided by the Overland Mail Company would "bind the

Pacific States more closely to the Union," and provide the nation with powerful ties.[7]

Lincoln's Inaugural Address

By March 1861, the problems between the North and the South were so severe that war seemed certain. In fact, seven Southern states had already left the Union and formed their own nation, the Confederate States of America. Despite the pledge California's government had made to support the Union, no one was sure which side California's population would take.

At the time, California was about evenly divided between former Northerners and Southerners. On top of that, there was a movement for California to leave the United States and become a separate nation. Even though they were thousands of miles away from the turmoil in the East, many Californians were deeply concerned about the outcome of the conflict between the North and the South.

Everyone knew that new President Abraham Lincoln was scheduled to make an inaugural address in March 1861. The position he took toward the growing crisis of Southern states leaving the Union could swing California to one side or another. All across the nation, people guessed about what he might say.

In the weeks before Lincoln's inaugural address, Russell, Majors & Waddell did everything possible to make certain its riders could make the best speed possible. The firm hired hundreds of extra employees and made certain to have more than enough horses at every station house along the way.

After Lincoln's speech on March 4, the Pony Express riders did not disappoint the firm. In only seven days and seventeen hours, Lincoln's inaugural address was in the hands of California newspaper editors. It had been the fastest trip ever for the Pony Express.

In his speech, Lincoln stated:

> In *your* hands, my dissatisfied fellow-countrymen, and not in *mine*, is the momentous issue of civil war. The Government will not assail *you*. You can have no conflict without being yourselves the aggressors. *You* have no oath registered in heaven to destroy the Government, while I shall have the most solemn one to "preserve, protect, and defend it."[8]

SOURCE DOCUMENT

APPREHENSION SEEMS TO EXIST AMONG THE PEOPLE OF THE SOUTHERN STATES THAT BY THE ASCENSION OF A REPUBLICAN ADMINISTRATION THEIR PROPERTY AND THEIR PEACE AND PERSONAL SECURITY ARE TO BE ENDANGERED. THERE HAS NEVER BEEN ANY REASONABLE CAUSE FOR SUCH APPREHENSION. . . . I TAKE THE OFFICIAL OATH TO-DAY WITH NO MENTAL RESERVATIONS AND WITH NO PURPOSE TO CONSTRUE THE CONSTITUTION OR LAWS BY ANY HYPERCRITICAL RULES. . . . I HOLD THAT IN CONTEMPLATION OF UNIVERSAL LAW AND OF THE CONSTITUTION OF THE UNION OF THESE IS PERPETUAL.[9]

Lincoln's address was carried with record speed to California by the riders of the Pony Express.

President Lincoln tried to encourage the Southern states to return to the Union with his inaugural address, which tried to show his belief that the Union could not be broken.

Californians were pleased with Lincoln's speech. And once again, the state pledged its loyalty to the Union.

The Transcontinental Telegraph

While Russell was using every opportunity to prove the value of the Pony Express, a new competitor was on the horizon. This one would surely make the Pony Express's service obsolete.

The United States government had signed contracts with two companies—the Pacific Telegraph Company and the Overland Telegraph Company—to build a telegraph line that stretched across the nation from coast to coast. The route that the transcontinental telegraph took was the same route used by the Pony Express.

In 1860, the first telegraph pole was set. On October 24, 1861, the last wires were connected near Salt Lake City, Utah. The transcontinental telegraph line was ready to go into service. Now, a message could be sent across the country in a matter of seconds. While the telegraph was being built, messages were carried by horse between Fort Kearny and Fort Churchill, but letters were carried by horse for the whole distance. The first telegraph message sent from California to the East was from Stephen J. Field, chief justice of the Supreme Court of California, to President Abraham Lincoln. It read:

To Abraham Lincoln, President of the United States: In the temporary absence of the Governor of the State, I am requested to send you the first message which will be transmitted over the wires of the telegraph line which connects the Pacific with the Atlantic States. The people of California desire to congratulate you upon the completion of the great work. . . . [T]hey desire in this—the first message across the continent— to express their loyalty to the Union and their determination to stand by its Government on this its day of trial. . . . —Stephen J. Field, Chief Justice of California.[10]

Once the transcontinental telegraph was in operation, the need for any kind of express mail delivery by horse riders greatly decreased. But while sending messages by telegraph was fast, it was also expensive. For the

In this illustration, a Pony Express rider raises a salute to the telegraph, which would eventually lead to the end of the Pony Express.

time being, most ordinary mail crossing the West would still be transported by the horse-drawn wagons of Butterfield's Overland Mail Company.

Farewell to the Pony Express

On October 26, 1861, newspapers in the West announced that Russell, Majors & Waddell was shutting down the Pony Express. However, letters that had already been mailed were delivered and riders in some regions of the West continued to make their runs until November 20.

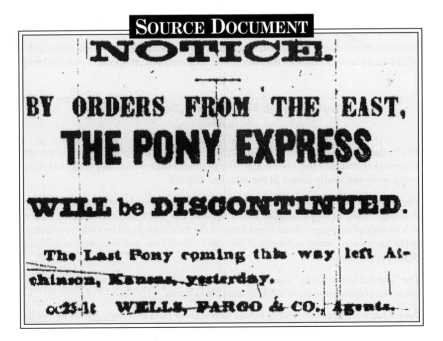

Newspapers and posters carried the news that the Pony Express, which had been the nation's great hope for the future of communication with the West, was going out of business after a year and a half.

As a financial enterprise, the Pony Express had been a total failure. No one knows exactly how much Russell invested in the service, but during its operation, the company only earned $90,141—about the cost of buying horses for the service.[11] One accountant who worked for the firm wrote, "The amount of business transacted was not sufficient to pay one-tenth of the expense."[12] In all, it is estimated that Russell and his partners had lost about $200,000 on the venture.

LEGACY OF THE PONY EXPRESS

During the year and a half the Pony Express was in operation, its riders traveled a total of over six hundred thousand miles, completed about three hundred mail runs, and carried more than thirty-three thousand pieces of mail. Approximately two thirds of the messages were sent from the West to the East. Each ride of the Pony Express brought news from family members, business communications, and sometimes even messages that were vital to the army or government officials.[1]

The Pony Express won the hearts of its customers like no other delivery service has ever done. It united the American nation at a time when the Civil War was tearing it apart. And it helped keep California and its gold in the Union.

A Tribute to the Pony Express

When the Pony Express closed, many western newspapers ran tributes to the service. One such article was published in the *Sacramento Bee*:

Our little friend, the Pony, is to run no more. "Stop it" is the order that has been issued by those in authority. Farewell and forever, thou staunch, wilderness-overcoming, swift-footed messenger. For the good thou hast done we praise thee. . . . Rest upon your honors; be satisfied with them, your destiny has been fulfilled—a new and higher power has superseded you. Nothing that has blood and sinews [muscles] was able to overcome your energy and ardor; but a senseless, soulless thing [the telegraph] that eats not, sleeps not, tires not—a thing that cannot distinguish space . . . has encompassed, overthrown and routed you.[2]

The Pony Express Remains Popular

Nearly a century and a half after the Pony Express was discontinued, it lives on as an American legend. Even when faster ways of transporting the mail became available, the Pony Express remained an important part of America's culture. Stories about well-known Pony Express riders often mixed fact with fiction to

An artist depicted the two main reasons—telegraph lines and railroad tracks—for the end of the Pony Express.

create unforgettable legends that appealed to the American sense of adventure.

Exaggerated tales of Indian attacks and gun battles with western bandits added excitement to traveling Wild West shows decades after the Pony Express closed. But these exaggerations were not really necessary to hold the public's attention. Pony Express riders' true acts of courage in the face of danger continued to inspire the imagination of Americans long after William Russell's company was forced to go out of business.

Riders Trace the Pony Express Route

Even today, Americans have a strong fascination with the Pony Express's colorful history. To commemorate the service the Pony Express once provided, members of the National Pony Express Association retrace the old Pony Express trail every year. For more than twenty years, members have ridden the trail between St. Joseph and Sacramento. Approximately five hundred men, women, and children come from all over the nation to participate. Every June, they carry the mail by horseback nearly two thousand miles. They make the trip in ten days and charge $5 to transport each letter, just as in the days of the Pony Express. Thanks to their efforts and the continuing development of the American West, the legacy of the Pony Express lives on.

★ TIMELINE ★

1848—The United States issues contracts for mail to be transported to California by steamship.

1849—Thousands of Americans go west in search of their fortune; Alexander Todd starts a one-man express service to deliver mail in the West.

1852—Henry Wells and William Fargo start an express service in California; Unlike the big freight companies, Wells-Fargo specializes in transporting mail, urgent dispatches, and gold and silver bullion.

1856—The Post Office Appropriations Bill is passed, calling for mail to be transported west by horse and wagon.

1857—John Butterfield wins the government contract to transport mail west via horse-drawn wagon; He starts the service a year later.

1859—William Russell and his business partners operate a mail route from Kansas to Colorado, called the Leavenworth and Pike's Peak Express.

1860—The Pony Express makes its first run on April 3, 1860; The Paiute War causes mail delivery to be delayed in the late spring; William Russell runs into financial problems; In late December, Russell is arrested for borrowing against securities that do not belong to him.

1861—Congress passes a law that authorizes mail service six days a week from Missouri to California; The $1,000,000-a-year mail contract is awarded to the Overland Mail company, founded by John Butterfield.

October 24: The transcontinental telegraph line is completed; Messages from the East can now be swiftly relayed to and from San Francisco by wire.
October 26: The Pony Express service is officially discontinued.

1862—Russell's company, including freight operations and mail contracts, is taken over by creditors because of loans Russell could not repay.

★ CHAPTER NOTES ★

Chapter 1. Here Comes the Pony Express!

1. Mark Twain, *Roughing It* (New York: Oxford University Press, 1996), pp. 71, 72.

2. Raymond W. Settle and Mary Lund Settle, *Saddles and Spurs: The Pony Express Saga* (Lincoln: University of Nebraska Press, 1972), p. 57.

Chapter 2. The Nation Expands to the West

1. Alvin F. Harlow, *Old Post Bags* (New York: D. Appleton and Company, 1928), p. 303.

2. Wayne E. Fuller, *The American Mail: Enlarger of the Common Life* (Chicago: University of Chicago Press, 1972), p. 87.

3. Henry Steele Commager, ed., *Documents of American History* (New York: Appleton-Century-Crofts, 1958), vol. 1, p. 212.

4. David Colbert, ed., *Eyewitness to America: 500 Years of America in the Words of Those Who Saw It Happen* (New York: Pantheon Books, 1997), p. 171.

5. F. M. Scanland, "Early Journalism in San Francisco," *Overland monthly* and *Out West* magazine, vol. 24, no. 141, September 1894, pp. 263–264.

6. Fuller, p. 97.

7. Harlow, p. 351.

8. Ray Allen Billington, *Westward Expansion: A History of the American Frontier,* 2nd ed. (New York: The McMillan Company, 1960), p. 635.

9. Marshall B. Davidson, *Life in America* (Boston: Houghton Mifflin Co., 1951), vol. 2, p. 259.

10. Ibid.

11. Raymond W. Settle and Mary Lund Settle, *Saddles and Spurs: The Pony Express Saga* (Lincoln: University of Nebraska Press, 1972), p. 19.

12. Fred Reinfeld, *Pony Express* (Lincoln: University of Nebraska Press, 1973), p. 19.

13. Settle and Settle, p. 19.

14. Edward Hungerford, *Wells Fargo: Advancing the American Frontier* (New York: Random House, 1949), pp. 37, 38.

Chapter 3. Mail Contracts to the West

1. Raymond W. Settle and Mary Lund Settle, *Saddles and Spurs: The Pony Express Saga* (Lincoln: University of Nebraska Press, 1972), p. 18.

2. Alvin F. Harlow, *Old Post Bags* (New York: D. Appleton and Company, 1928), p. 362.

3. Andrew Carroll, ed., *Letters of a Nation* (New York: Kodansha International, 1997), p. 22.

4. Settle and Settle, p. 20.

5. Ray Allen Billington, *Westward Expansion: A History of the American Frontier*, 2nd ed. (New York: The McMillan Company, 1960), p. 635.

6. Ralph Moody, *The Old Trails West* (New York: Thomas Y. Crowell Company, 1963), p. 293.

7. Harlow, p. 359.

8. Ibid., p. 361.

9. Horace Greeley, *An Overland Journey, from New York to San Francisco in the Summer of 1859* (New York: C. M. Saxton, Barker & Co; San Francisco, Calif.: H. H. Bancroft & Co, 1860), p. 371.

10. Ralph Moody, *Stagecoach West* (New York: Thomas Y. Crowell Company, 1967), p. 182.

Chapter 4. The Pony Express Is Established

1. Marshall B. Davidson, *Life in America* (Boston: Houghton Mifflin Co., 1951), vol. 2, p. 261.

2. Ibid.

3. Ibid., p. 260.

4. Horace Greeley, *An Overland Journey, from New York to San Francisco in the Summer of 1859* (New York: C. M. Saxton, Barker & Co; San Francisco, Calif.: H. H. Bancroft & Co, 1860), pp. 47–48.

5. Ralph Moody, *The Old Trails West* (New York: Thomas Y. Crowell Company, 1963), p. 293.

6. Ralph Moody, *Stagecoach West* (New York: Thomas Y. Crowell Company, 1967), p. 139.

7. R. Conrad Stein, *The Story of the Pony Express* (Chicago: Children's Press, 1981), p. 9.

8. Moody, *Stagecoach West*, p. 141.

9. Will Bagley, *Pony Express National Historic Trail Brochure*, 1998, n.p.

10. Richard Francis Burton, *The city of the saints, and across the Rocky mountains to California* (New York: Harper and Brothers, 1862), p. 29.

11. Roy S. Bloss, *Pony Express—The Great Gamble* (Berkeley, Calif.: Howell-North Press, 1959), p. 95.

Chapter 5. The First Ride of the Pony Express

1. Raymond W. Settle and Mary Lund Settle, *Saddles and Spurs: The Pony Express Saga* (Lincoln: University of Nebraska Press, 1972), p. 57.

2. Mayor M. Jeff Thomas's speech in front of Patee House on April 3, 1860, Courtesy of Gary Chilcote, director of the Patee House Museum.

3. Settle and Settle, p. 56.

4. Fred Reinfeld, *Pony Express* (Lincoln: University of Nebraska Press, 1973), pp. 56, 57.

5. Ibid., p. 57.

6. Settle and Settle, 60.

7. Reinfeld, p. 63.

8. Ralph Moody, *The Old Trails West* (New York: Thomas Y. Crowell Company, 1963), p. 296.

9. Malcolm Keir, *The March of Commerce*, ed. Ralph Henry Gabriel, *The Pageant of America* (New York: Oxford University Press, 1952), vol. 4, p. 163.

Chapter 6. The Lives of Pony Express Riders

1. Mark Twain, *Roughing It* (New York: Oxford University Press, 1996), p. 70.

2. Library of Congress, *American Memory*, n.d., <http://www.loc.gov> (August 14, 2000).

3. Will Bagley, *Pony Express National Historic Trail Brochure*, 1998, n.p.

4. Henry T. Williams, *The Pacific Tourist* (New York: H. T. Williams, Publisher, 1876), p. 42.

5. Malcolm Keir, *The March of Commerce*, ed. Ralph Henry Gabriel, *The Pageant of America* (New York: Oxford University Press, 1952), vol. 4, p. 163.

6. Fred Reinfeld, *Pony Express* (Lincoln: University of Nebraska Press, 1973), p. 72.

7. Richard Francis Burton, *The City of the Saints, and across the Rocky Mountains to California* (New York: Harper and Brothers, 1862), p. 28.

8. Ibid.

Chapter 7. The Final Months of the Pony Express

1. Raymond W. Settle and Mary Lund Settle, *Saddles and Spurs: The Pony Express Saga* (Lincoln: University of Nebraska Press, 1972), p. 32.

2. Ralph Moody, *Stagecoach West* (New York: Thomas Y. Crowell Company, 1967), p. 186.

3. Ibid., p. 187.

4. Dee Brown, *The Westerners* (New York: Holt, Rinehart and Winston, 1974), p. 164.

5. Settle and Settle, p. 177.

6. Edward Hungerford, *Wells Fargo: Advancing the American Frontier* (New York: Random House, 1949), p. 86.

7. Wayne E. Fuller, *The American Mail: Enlarger of the Common Life* (Chicago: University of Chicago Press, 1972), p. 100.

8. Abraham Lincoln, *Inaugural Address*, <http://www.bartleby.com/124/pres31.html> (October 18, 2000).

9. Jerome B. Agel, ed., *Words That Make America Great* (New York: Random House, 1997), pp. 196, 197.

10. Howard R. Driggs, *The Pony Express Goes Through* (New York: Frederick A. Stokes Company, 1935), pp. 57, 58.

11. Tom Crews, *Pony Express Home Station Bunkhouse Web Site*, <http://www.xphomestation.com/frm-history.html> (October 11, 2000).

12. R. Conrad Stein, *The Story of the Pony Express* (Chicago: Children's Press, 1981), p. 30.

Chapter 8. Legacy of the Pony Express

1. Tom Crews, *Pony Express Home Station Bunkhouse Web Site*, <http://www.xphomestation.com/frm-history.html> (October 11, 2000).

2. Dee Brown, *The Westerners* (New York: Holt, Rinehart and Winston, 1974), p. 166.

★ FURTHER READING ★

Altman, Linda Jacobs. *The California Gold Rush in American History.* Springfield, N.J.: Enslow Publishers, Inc., 1997.

Peters, Arthur King. *Seven Trails West.* New York: Abbeville Press, Inc., 1996.

Settle, Raymond W., and Mary Lund Settle. *Saddles and Spurs: The Pony Express Saga.* Lincoln: University of Nebraska Press, 1972.

Stein, R. Conrad. *The Story of the Pony Express.* Chicago: Children's Press, 1981.

———. *The Transcontinental Railroad in American History.* Springfield, N.J.: Enslow Publishers, Inc., 1997.

★ INTERNET ADDRESSES ★

Crews, Tom. *Pony Express Home Station Bunkhouse.* June 1997. <http://www.xphomestation.com>.

Pony Express Historical Association. March 14, 1997. <http://stjoseph.net/ponyexpress/>.

"Pony Express Information." *American West.* 1996. <http://www.americanwest.com/trails/pages/ponyexp1.htm>.

"Pony Express." *Museum of the City of San Francisco.* n.d. <http://www.sfmuseum.org/hist1/pxpress.html>.

Pony Express Museum, St. Joseph, Mo. n.d. <http://www.ponyexpress.org>.

★ INDEX ★

A

Alta Telegraph, 56–57
Antelope, 57, 59
Apache Indians, 31

B

Baily, Godard, 79, 80
Brodhead, Richard, 16–17
Buchanan, James, 75–76
Burton, Richard Francis, 46,
  72–73
Butterfield, John, 7, 28, 29,
  30, 31, 32, 72, 75, 81

C

Calhoun, John, 9–10
California Gold Rush. *See*
  gold rush.
Californian, 15
Central Overland Route, 38,
  75–76, 81
Civil War, 7, 82–83, 85–86,
  89
Clark, Ad, 53
Comanche Indians, 31

D

Davis, George H., 53
Davis, Jefferson, 18
Delano, Alonzo, 20

F

Field, Stephen J., 85–86
Floyd, John B., 78–79
Fry, Johnny, 54

G

gold rush, 14–16, 36
Great American Desert, 11
Greeley, Horace, 33

Gwin, William, 34, 35, 40,
  75

H

Hamilton, Sam, 57, 58
Hannibal and St. Joseph
  Railroad, 52–53
Haslam, "Pony" Bob, 69–71
Hockaday and Liggett, 25
Holt, Joseph, 32–33

I

Indian Bond Scandal, 78–79,
  80–81
Indian Trust Bonds, 79
Interior Department, 79

K

Kickapoo Indians, 54
Kiowa Indians, 31

L

Lincoln, Abraham, 76, 78,
  82–83, 85–86

M

Madison, James, 10, 11
Majors, Alexander, 28, 36,
  39–40, 41, 44, 45, 47,
  48, 88
Marshall, James, 14
Missouri, 53
mochila, 47, 63
Mormons, 41–42, 68

N

National Pony Express
  Association, 91
New York Sun, 53
New York Tribune, 33, 53

O

Overland Mail Company, 28, 30, 81–82
Overland Telegraph Company, 85
Ox Bow Route, 7, 29, 37, 75

P

Pacific Telegraph Company, 85
Paiute Indians, 69–72
Paiute War, 62, 69–72
Patee House, 51
Pony Express riders' oath, 47, 49
Post Office Appropriations Bill, 28
Post Route Bill, 81

R

Randall, James, 57
relay stations, 66–67
Russell, Majors & Waddell, 25–26, 29, 37, 42–43, 45, 46, 47, 50, 51, 65, 67, 72, 74, 75, 78, 81, 82–83, 87, 88
Russell, William H., 28, 29, 34, 35, 36, 37, 38, 39–41, 44, 47, 59, 60, 71, 74, 75, 78–79, 80–81, 88

S

Sacramento Bee, 89
San Francisco Bulletin, 34
station houses, 65, 66, 67
Sutter, John, 14
Sutter's Mill, 14, 15

T

Taylor, William, 17
telegraph, 52, 72–73, 76, 85–87
Thompson, M. Jeff, 52
Todd, Alexander H., 18–20
transcontinental railroad, 32–33
Twain, Mark, 5–6, 60

U

United States Treasury, 10
Upson, "Boston", 58

W

Waddell, William B., 28, 36, 39–41, 44, 74, 75, 88
Wells, Fargo & Company, 20–22
Woodson, Samuel, 24–25